The Future of Learning for Work

The Chartered Institute of Personnel and Development is the leading publisher of books and reports for personnel and training professionals, students, and all those concerned with the effective management and development of people at work. For full details of all our titles, please contact the Publishing Department:

Tel: 020 8263 3387
Fax: 020 8263 3850

E-mail: publish@cipd.co.uk

The catalogue of all CIPD titles can be viewed on the CIPD website:
www.cipd.co.uk/publications

The Future of Learning for Work

David Wilson
Elizabeth Lank
Andy Westwood
Ewart Keep
Charles Leadbeater
Martyn Sloman

First published 2001

Cover design by Curve
Designed and typeset by Beacon GDT
Printed in Great Britain by the Short Run Press, Exeter

British Library Cataloguing in Publication Data
A catalogue record for this book is available from the British Library

ISBN 0 85292 934 X

Chartered Institute of Personnel and Development,
CIPD House, Camp Road, London SW19 4UX

Tel: 020 8971 9000
Fax: 020 8263 3333
Website: www.cipd.co.uk

Incorporated by Royal Charter. Registered charity no. 1079797.

Contents

Acknowledgements

The CIPD would like to thank Phillip Hadridge for leading the contributor workshop in April 2001 and Louise Horner of the Performance and Innovation Unit for her participation in and contribution to the workshop.

Foreword

In the knowledge economy everyone has a stake in learning – it underpins individual, organisational and national competitiveness. Everyone benefits from a workforce that has continuous opportunities to learn, builds on prior learning in a focused and systematic way and is motivated to learn. But how might people's experience of learning for work change in the future?

The CIPD is exploring how the balance of responsibility for learning between the employee, employers and government might shift and what these changes will mean for the individual learner. To do this, we invited six commentators to attend a workshop in order to discuss which critical issues will shape the future of learning for work. These issues included the following.

Role of companies and organisations

- the link between learning and organisational competitiveness
- the impact of economic slowdowns or recessions on how and how much organisations provide learning.

Role of government

- the coherence of government strategies in co-ordinating national, individual and business learning needs
- the imposition of standards – before or after supply-side innovation.

Role of individual learners

- the role of learning brands and the learner as a consumer – will the learner become an increasingly sophisticated consumer able to choose exactly the right kind of learning for his or her needs, or will the learner be 'dumbed down' and blindly choose the most popular and extensively marketed learning brands regardless of quality or suitability?
- the individuals' own awareness of job entry currency – how will this change and develop?
- the impact of 'star syndrome' and the 'winner-takes-all' economy – how will star performers influence work structures and patterns?

The overall context

- the continuing persistence of the low skill equilibrium
- the structure of the economy and the balance between so-called 'good' and 'bad' jobs
- changing attitudes towards work and technology, either through learners becoming more receptive to technology or, conversely, a backlash against it

- improvements in technology and e-learning provision
- the differentiation of the workforce into those (mainly knowledge) workers who build their identities around their work and those who think of work as simply a 'means to an end'.

We then invited the commentators to offer their own vision of what the future might hold. All agree that the future of learning seems to lie in the uncertainties. Revolutionary changes in technology will change the way we learn. E-learning has inspired organisations and, in some cases, nations to think ambitiously and to re-evaluate how learning is delivered on a grand scale. The incredible options that e-learning offers – possibilities that we can now see at work in large corporations – provoke a whole new set of questions. Employees in these types of organisation will enjoy enriched learning experiences, but what about those who do not work in this type of environment? What other options will there be beyond this corporate brand of learning? Will high-quality learning ever be freely available to everyone? How might this develop? Or will it become even more difficult for individuals to get access to the kind of knowledge that promises more opportunities and better wages because the most valuable learning experiences will not be those provided publicly by governments but rather those provided by corporations?

The contributions to this publication aim to explore future possibilities, but it is important to remember that they are not meant to be predictions. They are simply a way of thinking about the individual's experience of learning for work and employability in the future based on the authors' thoughts about:

- what could happen
- what they'd like to see happening
- what they fear might happen.

We have a lot to learn about learning itself, and we have aimed at making a start in examining some of these issues and seeing where they take us. The CIPD will continue to encourage further debate on this important subject and to support the search for learning solutions that will provide the architecture for future success and competitiveness.

Jennifer Schramm

Adviser, Training and Development
Chartered Institute of Personnel and Development

Executive summary

Chapter 1

Reinventing learning within business
David Wilson

David Wilson, managing director of independent e-learning consultancy eLearnity, explores some of the key shifts taking place within the workplace and looks ahead to see how these changes will affect business processes, the role of the learner and the future of learning delivery within companies.

Chapter 2

From learning at work to workplaces that learn – can we develop intelligent organisations?
Elizabeth Lank

Elizabeth Lank, an independent consultant, author and knowledge management expert, examines how 'the intelligent organisation' will look and what this could mean for the way companies attract talented employees, as well as the way people work and interact with each other within organisations.

Chapter 3

Drawing a line – who is going to train our workforce?
Andy Westwood

Andy Westwood, head of policy research at the Industrial Society, looks at how current work-based learning practice could mean a further deepening of the divided economy. He argues that UK employer and government training expenditure will need to make a dramatic shift in favour of lower earners, low and unskilled workers, part-time workers and others on the fringes of the labour market in order to remain competitive.

Chapter 4

The skills system in 2015
Ewart Keep

Ewart Keep, deputy director of SKOPE, the ESRC Research Centre on Skills, Knowledge and Organisational Performance, uses a future scenario to demonstrate how the UK's national training strategy might shift away from a traditionally framed skills policy and training system to a more co-ordinated approach where workforce learning is integrated into a broader productivity and competitiveness strategy.

Chapter 5
Learning and work: authorship
Charles Leadbeater

Charles Leadbeater, an independent writer and policy adviser, unpacks the concept of authorship – what makes it a distinctive and important factor in the new economy, what value it will hold for individual workers and their careers, and how people can learn to acquire it.

Chapter 6
Sharing the power of learning
Martyn Sloman

Martyn Sloman, CIPD adviser, training and development and author of *The E-Learning Revolution* (CIPD, 2001), explores how the open-source software movement may signal a way forward for learners by widening access and building learning communities that shift power away from providers and back into the hands of the learners themselves.

David Wilson is a leading speaker and commentator on e-learning within Europe. David has authored a number of leading strategy documents and White Papers on e-learning, is a frequent contributor to e-learning articles and magazine columns, and a leading speaker at e-learning conferences.

In 1996, David founded and is managing director of eLearnity, Europe's leading independent e-learning consultancy. With over five years' in-depth experience, including many e-learning projects, eLearnity has developed a unique understanding of the e-learning marketplace and technologies, and is a leader in e-learning methodology and best practice.

Prior to founding eLearnity, David was the principal consultant for the groupware and Internet businesses of QA Training, the largest independent IT training company in the UK. David was a leading exponent of how the Internet would transform business and working practice, and spoke at many conferences and seminars in the USA and Europe. As part of this role, David also sat on the worldwide Education Advisory Council for Lotus Development. Before joining QA, David held a variety of senior positions in IT consulting and software organisations, focusing on advanced technologies and business transformation.

1 | Reinventing learning within business

David Wilson

Introduction

The business of learning is changing – change creates opportunity and imposes threats. Learning and knowledge have probably never been higher on the corporate agenda. As the percentage of value delivered tangibly shifts from physical to knowledge 'value-add', and as continuous, increasing change becomes the accepted norm, the need to continuously learn and evolve is becoming a fundamental requirement for organisations, for teams and for individuals.

As well as macro-factors – economic and competitive – affecting the need for learning, there are also some key micro ones. Training and development has been one of the last bastions of traditionalism in the corporate world. Reviewing the focus and activities of a corporate training function will probably show little real change. Running courses, classrooms and instructors has changed little as a business over the last 10 or 20 years. But all that is changing.

I explore here some of the key shifts taking place within the context of learning for work and within work. My focus in this broad discussion is on what happens to the learner within companies rather than what happened before joining them. Whilst much of the macro-level focus seems to be on the state's role in preparing people for their life in work (including secondary and tertiary education), or on such areas as retraining once their current work has finished, my belief is that beyond some high-level influences on macro-competitiveness, the real issues of learning for work need to be tackled and considered within the context of work itself, or more fundamentally, within the context of employment. Once you've entered the work system, it is learning within that system that really determines the value-add.

Physical to knowledge economy

So let's consider learning within work, and in particular some of the major shifts taking place. I have already mentioned one of the macro-level factors affecting business, the shift from physical to knowledge value-add – that is, the rise of the knowledge economy. I would argue that this change has significant consequences for our concepts of learning for work. What does the knowledge value-add really mean in terms of companies, for the kinds of job within companies and for individuals?

First, the kinds of job within companies are changing, shifting as one would expect towards knowledge working rather than physical working. This has massive implications in terms of skills and learning. The proportion of jobs has shifted significantly during the past 20 or 30 years from blue collar to white collar, from manufacturing to service, and from factory to office. Now the structure of white-collar office jobs is also changing, with corporate restructuring, re-engineering, and outsourcing.

'The loss of the "job for life" in the restructuring of the 1990s has shifted the responsibility for employability away from the company to the individual.'

Whilst the big guys are getting bigger, underneath them and within them there is a fragmentation and explosion in small and independent businesses; the middle is getting squeezed. The loss of the 'job for life' in the restructuring of the 1990s has shifted the responsibility for employability away from the company to the individual. Technology has then further fanned the flames and is starting to enable homeworking to become a real white-collar option, and for valuable knowledge workers to leave their companies to become independent consultants or form their own micro-companies. Charles and Elizabeth Handy have an interesting way of discussing this phenomenon – he talks about elephants and fleas.[1] The elephants may be getting bigger, but the fleas now increasingly control the means of production – themselves. This is leading to changes in the relationships between employers and employees and the growth in the star-worker syndrome.

Reinventing yourself

Traditionally, learning for work has been something that's done to you. Your involvement tends to be as passive receiver. When you start in a specific job or role you get put onto specific courses associated with your job role as well as initial induction training on the company. As you develop your experience, additional learning requirements are identified as part of your career development and personal appraisal process. Once you become competent and experienced, the level of explicit learning activity decreases significantly and job-role-based requirements are replaced with managerial or leadership training.

This traditional development model is becoming increasingly challenged. You no longer have one primary career or job role as you develop through your lifetime. Studies talk about individuals having at least three careers and many more employers in their working lifetime. From a career perspective, learning is not something you need to do at the start of your career, but is something you will do repeatedly – sometimes incrementally, sometimes radically to reflect bigger shifts in your employability. With the rate of change in business, products and technology still increasing, the magnitude of this challenge is ever greater.

The rise of 'e'

Of course, the other big change is due to technology and, more importantly, the potential for technology to change and reinvent the model. As well as the external structural changes taking place, as discussed previously, there are equally significant internal structural changes as well. Let's think in terms of the customer of the learning processes – the learner – and think about the changes in the way he or she will engage with learning in the future.

We have already discussed a shift in responsibility for learning – away from the corporation and towards the individual. This shift has been further accelerated by the ability for technology to provide self-service interfaces to learning in all forms. The rapid growth in e-learning as a viable and increasingly vital part of the learning process will continue. Looking ahead over the next 10–20 years, I think it's very difficult to imagine any kind of mainstream model of corporate learning and development that is close to the way it's done today, which in most cases is not that far removed from the way it was done 10 or 20 years ago – in classrooms.

Once upon a time...

Let's try to articulate this more clearly in the form of a discussion of a potential scenario. Let's consider a large UK-centric company with some overseas operations. The company will change quite a lot over the coming years. First of all, it merges with a slightly smaller European rival, forming a stronger pan-European company. Then a couple of years later it is itself acquired by a US-based competitor, forming one of the top three global players in its market. There is tremendous internal change associated with these mergers and acquisitions. Manufacturing and business operations are rationalised into a smaller number of larger centres; business administration is centralised, losing at least one of the headquarters offices. The number of products and brands is also rationalised alongside direct sales force and partners and resellers.

In the meantime, the external market continues to move on rapidly. Other competitors are also going through their own mergers and acquisitions. The rate of new product introduction continues to increase, and the predicted life span of individual products is decreasing. Europe has overtaken the USA as the largest geographical market, and Asia Pacific is growing fast. Research and development and marketing costs continue to grow as a proportion of total cost base whilst manufacturing decreases.

In the space of a few years, both the company and the products have changed fundamentally following merger and acquisition activity. With business operations merging, staff at all levels need to rapidly become competent with the new products, new markets, new customers and new ways of doing business. The proportion of staff continues to shift away from production and manufacturing and towards knowledge workers. Research, marketing and customer service functions grow as a proportion of total employees. Business administration and financial operations are restructured multiple times, with many office-based redundancies.

And for learning...

From a learning and development perspective, the changes are huge. The merging of the three original businesses leads to the formation of a single corporate learning and development (L&D) organisation – now given a remit to co-ordinate all learning activities across the company. Overall, training budgets are reduced in line with the merging of the training functions – even though the amount of training is clearly on the increase. L&D works together with HR to develop and implement a core competency framework defining the main competencies and roles across the organisation. This is rolled out in a piece-meal way across the main business functions and geographies, and over time is implemented across the whole business. The HR focus on competencies is also associated with a shift towards a 'performance culture' and more active ways of measuring and managing performance at an organisational and individual level. New forms of assessment are introduced to focus more on performance and work-based measures as well as more comprehensive forms of career planning, personal assessment and development objectives.

Portals and programmes

L&D implements a global learning portal on the company's (now global) intranet. This is universally available and provides access to all forms of learning across the company regardless of region or subject matter. For the first time, L&D gets access to comprehensive management information on all forms of learning activity and expenditure across the company. Whilst initially the focus is on making existing courses and learning offers available, increasingly L&D rationalises the learning offer to focus activity on programmes associated with core competencies. The overall number of courses and programmes is reduced as overlaps and low-value activities are removed.

The core programmes are used to drive the primary competencies and performance culture into the organisation, and used to reinforce the structural changes in the business, its markets and products. Rather than individual courses, they become a series of learning and development events over a longer elapsed time, maybe 12–18 months. Whereas originally the audiences for these programmes were geographically based (from their original organisations), now they are global programmes with attendees from anywhere. Increasing pressure on travel and subsistence budgets and a need to maximise the value of face-to-face time lead to a restructuring of the delivery into an integrated learning model.

In these programmes, e-learning is used for initial self-paced knowledge transfer and online assessments to ensure attendees have the appropriate prerequisite knowledge for the face-to-face events. This enables increasing focus within face-to-face delivery onto application of the knowledge and behavioural change. Assignments become increasingly work-based, with remote support and coaching provided by live and asynchronous e-learning technology. Assessment is tied back into performance measures and competencies, and integrated into their appropriate systems.

Overall the balance of learning activity has shifted away from mainly classroom to a mix of face-to-face, e-learning and technology-supported workplace activity. This will be delivered using a mix of internal and external specialists, and custom and generic materials as appropriate.

Learning on demand

Outside core programmes, L&D provides access to an increasing number of just-in-time courses or learning objects to cover a big range of topics inside and outside the business, including business skills, personal skills, information technology and so on. These courses become smaller and are designed to deliver very specific skills or knowledge around a particular problem. Increasingly these are delivered using e-learning as the only viable way of reaching individuals when they need it. But e-learning here means more than online, Web-based content. Self-paced content has a role, and there is an increasing amount of generic learning objects in the marketplace that could be made available to staff on a just-in-time basis. But the uniqueness of company-specific knowledge and the need to allow other forms of learning other than self-paced results in the need to enable peer-to-peer learning on demand, ie as well as accessing content on demand, L&D also provides an infrastructure to connect people to experts on demand. This is more challenging but also potentially a significantly more valuable model.

'...the balance of learning activity has shifted away from mainly classroom to a mix of face-to-face, e-learning and technology-supported workplace activity.'

Me, the learner?

From the learners' perspective, they have access to a much more comprehensive set of learning options that are more focused around their needs and their longer-term development. The learning portal provides the window into this new world of learning. As well as providing ways of seeing and searching what is available, the portal also provides direct links into HR and performance systems, enabling learners to manage their personal development plans and assess competencies and needs against learning and development alternatives. Most importantly it gives learners control over their own learning and development. This shift in control is further reinforced through the implementation of personal learning accounts, actually giving learners some budgetary control over what they need or buy.

The flip-side of this shift in control is that the management systems are now in place to automatically manage approvals for learning requests, and the management information is available for learning by individual, team, organisation and function. This information brings much greater visibility and individual and management accountability for learning spend. Tying it back into performance and development objectives gives much greater accountability for the process of learning itself.

And the reality?

Looking at many companies today, we can see these changes starting to take place. There has been a significant growth in interest in areas of e-HR as well as e-learning, and increasingly these are being tied together. Learning programmes are being tied into competency frameworks, and competencies are being tied into performance measures. E-learning is growing rapidly as a viable delivery model, and there has been much interest recently in the concept of blended or integrated learning programmes.

In technology terms, there is still a big investment needed in underlying infrastructure, such as global intranets, increasing network bandwidth and implementing global systems for managing operations and HR. We have seen rapid growth in technologies to support e-learning – for access and management, for delivery in a variety of forms and for content. There has been significant activity around learning management systems (LMSs) as a core component of the e-learning infrastructure to manage and provide access to learning in all forms – classroom and e-learning.

As well as significant growth in the number of e-learning courses available in the generic marketplace, there has been an explosion on the supply side of the industry. Virtually every training company seems to have its own e-learning story, even if it is still limited in terms of its real e-learning experience and products. The e-learning marketplace is starting to mature, and companies are merging and acquiring as well as growing organically. They are also starting to acquire traditional classroom training businesses as they leverage their relatively higher market capitalisation to aggressively grow revenues and develop end-to-end solutions.

Work is changing and learning is changing with it, including:

- the increasing rate of change in business
- the shift to knowledge workers and knowledge working

- trends towards even larger, more distributed global companies and smaller, more dynamic knowledge worker units
- the increasing power and viability of technology as a universal communication and delivery platform.

Are all contributing to drive change into the learning marketplace? As well as general growth in the formal importance of learning within business, we are starting to see:

- a shift in responsibility for learning from the corporation to the individual
- a restructuring of learning delivery away from courses to developmental learning programmes, learning on demand and learning communities
- development of centralised mechanisms for providing access to and management of learning
- restructuring of learning delivery away from classroom-only models to integrated/blended learning models
- a rapid growth in the use of e-learning delivery components
- increasing use of work-based assessment and developmental objectives managed and facilitated remotely using technology-based mechanisms.

The shift has started to take place. Looking forward 10 or 20 years, it is hard to see how this will not emerge as a dominant shift, transforming the shape of corporate learning and development forever.

Endnote

1 HANDY C. *and* HANDY E. (1999) *The New Alchemists*. London, Hutchinson.

Elizabeth Lank is an independent consultant, speaker and author whose expertise lies in helping organisations to develop new ways of working to meet the demands of the twenty-first century. She has a particular interest in helping leaders to harness knowledge as a business asset. Her commitment to this aspect of business leadership comes from nearly five years of practical implementation experience from leading a major knowledge management initiative across a large multinational (ICL).

Prior to taking on her Mobilising Knowledge role, which developed over time to include responsibility for internal communications and people development, Elizabeth was head of management development at ICL. A Canadian by birth, she graduated *cum laude* from Mount Holyoke College in Massachusetts in 1980 and completed the INSEAD MBA programme in 1986.

Elizabeth is co-author of the book *The Power of Learning* (IPD 1994). She has published a number of articles on knowledge management and collaborated with Amin Rajan on the research report *Good Practices in Knowledge Creation and Exchange* (CREATE 1998). She is a member of the international editorial boards of the *Journal of Knowledge Management* and *Knowledge Management Review,* and has written a monthly column for *Human Resources* magazine on the implementation challenges of knowledge management.

2 | From learning at work to workplaces that learn – can we develop intelligent organisations?

Elizabeth Lank

In today's business world it is common practice for individuals to have to undergo various types of psychometric test to assess their suitability for a role. Looking ahead a few years, potential employees will turn the tables on employers. In a world where the competition for skills will be intense, people will be assessing the IQ of the organisation that wishes to employ them before they commit themselves to joining it.

They will judge whether the organisation has learned to learn – or, to put it another way, whether it knows what it knows. Here are some of the questions they will ask:

- How long does it take to find the company experts on a particular subject?
- When you find them, how readily do they help you?
- Does your organisation have established information services and processes that support employees with information needs?
- Can you get a complete picture of all the work you have done with your customers and the relevant contact names?
- Is there a process for capturing lessons learned after pieces of work are completed?
- Do you provide an office environment that facilitates communication, ie open plan with plenty of comfortable meeting areas?
- Will my induction programme cover all the things I need to know to be effective quickly in the organisation, including what knowledge and experience are available to support me in my role?

- What communication processes do you have to keep me updated on company and professional matters?

Potential employees will know that their own skills and marketability will be affected by the answers that an employer provides to these questions. Access to knowledge and information and opportunities to learn will be as high on a potential employee's priority list as salary and benefits. Terms like 'learning organisation' or one of the latest buzzwords, 'knowledge management', are sometimes dismissed as temporary management fads or fuzzy concepts that don't translate into hard business benefit. Yet the ability to harness learning will be critical to both winning business and attracting and retaining employees. The question is: how do you develop that capability as a core competence of an organisation?

'...if teamwork and collaboration are not core values, then the organisational brain will never develop to competitive levels.'

Identifying knowledge assets

Just as an individual makes choices in terms of where to invest his or her personal learning time, an organisation can afford to invest only in areas of knowledge and expertise that directly support its business aims. Making some conscious choices and then mobilising knowledge around them should be core to any business strategy. Intelligent organisations will know what knowledge is critical to their business and will make it clear to employees. If employees gain some useful knowledge, they will know who to feed it to and how.

Incentives to share

Individuals learn better when there is real motivation to learn. Perhaps they are motivated by career progression or the opportunity to move into a new area of interest. It is usually quite clear to individuals why they should invest time in learning for themselves – but why should they spend time helping their organisation learn? If you were the expert contacted by a colleague to help put a customer proposal together, what would be your incentive to help?

These questions must be answered in order for organisational learning to be sustained. If you think about the reasons for which you might help a colleague, they are rarely to do with financial incentive. Appreciation is a big motivator. Good relationships help – you are more likely to help a friend than an acquaintance. Give and take is also a factor – if you believe you will one day have the favour returned, you are more likely to help. Intelligent organisations will formalise this to a greater degree, for example by using peer appraisal systems to assess whether people readily share their expertise with colleagues – which might then have a direct effect on their career progression.

Organisational learning depends on individuals being willing to collaborate with their colleagues – if teamwork and collaboration are not core values, then the organisational brain will never develop to competitive levels. Intelligent organisations will know this and invest significant time and effort in fostering good relationships between people in the organisation.

Learning from experience

The informal sharing that happens when a colleague asks for help is one aspect of organisational learning and will be encouraged. However, just as an organisation often doesn't know what it knows, individuals might not know what they know either. Having completed a challenging customer project, perhaps over many months, you might expect that the lessons an individual or team learns in that process would be harvested for the good of the organisation. Yet it is not that simple. Without clear processes to harvest the 'knowledge yield' from any business effort, there is a danger that real nuggets of learning remain in people's heads, invisible even to them. Effective facilitation can bring these to light, such as the after-action reviews pioneered by the US Army or the peer reviews championed by oil company BP. Institutionalising these can make a world of difference to the IQ of the organisation.

The intelligent organisation will have defined processes for harvesting the learning from business actions. Managers will see time spent on learning reviews as core to the business, not as a 'nice-to-have' option that can be traded for other things. When lessons learned are identified, individuals will be made accountable for implementing the implications of those lessons, eg process changes.

Knowledge communities

Learning from experience is one of the key ways that an organisation develops its capability to act intelligently – but it is not just in relation to one business activity that lessons can be learned. Every organisation has communities of people spread across many business areas who have similar learning needs. These may be professional communities – people who need similar professional skill development to serve the organisation well. Or they may be communities of interest, such as people following a new development in the market and looking to maximise the business opportunity from it. Or they may be project teams or account teams who all want to keep up to date on developments with that project or customer. One of the interesting characteristics of these knowledge-sharing communities is that they rarely appear on organisation charts – they generally cross many organisational boundaries. They need to be nurtured without being stifled, as they are at their most effective when populated by willing volunteers.

The willingness to invest in these dynamic communities that no one part of the organisation can own is another feature of an effective learning organisation. In the intelligent organisation, the senior management group will be aware of these invisible structures and will support them with encouragement and resources.

Tools for the job

Facilitating knowledge and information flows across the organisation needs more than just willing individuals – certain tools enable the whole process to be efficient and affordable on a global scale. These tools include different types of information systems: e-mail, telephones, video conference facilities, voice mail facilities. This complex web of information channels forms what Bill Gates dubbed the 'digital nervous system' of the organisation. It is not that these tools hold the organisation's knowledge – but they help to channel it. The information available on computer systems is often a vital memory aid, an antidote to corporate amnesia. Yet it is primarily a signpost to where the knowledge is held, namely in people. When faced with the option of wading through a 20-page lessons-learned document or having a half-hour conversation with the person who wrote it, most people would prefer the latter. Technology tools can ensure that you connect with the right person for that half-hour conversation much faster than would otherwise have been possible – indeed you might never have found them otherwise.

The winning company of the future will help people get comfortable with the technology tools available to help them access the organisation's knowledge and experience. Its employees will know which tools are best for which purpose. Information will be presented in ways that make it easy to find and reuse. This will be achieved because the business will treat information as a business asset, that is with clear accountabilities (sometimes full-time, sometimes part-time) for maintaining and developing the organisation's information base.

Tried and tested

There are some very well-established knowledge-transfer mechanisms that need to be seen again from this new-found knowledge perspective. Training and development, coaching, mentoring, internal communication processes – these continue to be valuable ways of formally transferring knowledge from one part of the organisation to the next. They may not be digital but they are still part of the nervous system – still transmitters and receivers of critical knowledge and experience. An induction course can be seen as a straightforward administrative HR responsibility – or it can be viewed as the first opportunity to introduce an individual to the collective wisdom of the organisation that he or she has just joined. The sooner an individual is connected to the organisation's brain, the more quickly he or she will contribute to business success. Yet how often does induction get the attention it deserves? So often it is still 'sink or swim' – you know your way to the car park and how to fill out the holiday forms but how to tap into the organisation's knowledge base is left for you to work out.

The intelligent organisation of the future will use training programmes as an opportunity to transfer best practice as well as develop skills. Individuals and teams with experience will be moved to where their knowledge and experience are needed, when they are needed. Newcomers will be treated as apprentices, with more experienced people there to support them, especially in their first few months with the organisation.

The physical environment

People sharing knowledge and experience need as many opportunities to connect as possible. We have talked about some of the formal processes and tools that enable this to happen. But much valuable and creative interchange between people occurs spontaneously – in a corridor conversation, around the water cooler, over a cup of coffee. These unplanned exchanges can be considerably multiplied if the physical working environment enables them to happen. Barriers such as office walls and cubicle screens get in the way. Open-spaces, numerous meeting rooms, coffee corners, relaxed seating areas – these are the physical signs of an organisation that is looking to seize every available opportunity to marshal its collective wisdom. Open-plan offices are not everyone's preferred way of working, but combined with the availability of quiet areas for thinking time, they vastly increase the chances of people knowing what is going on and keeping up to date as the business evolves day to day.

Successful organisations will design their offices for knowledge work. Open-plan work areas, with significant space dedicated to helping groups of people work together effectively, will be the norm, along with comfortable coffee areas and restaurants that are open all day as informal meeting areas. These features will not be seen as an unnecessary expense – they will be seen as an essential investment to support a collaborative way of working.

'The intelligent organisation of the future will use training programmes as an opportunity to transfer best practice as well as develop skills.'

The nightmare scenario

Let's return to a more common picture – one of an organisation operating significantly below its potential. There is no expertise register of who knows what around the company. Lessons are learned and then lost because there is no process to capture and share them. Induction and training get little investment and managers generally only pay lip-service to the topic of personal development. The office environment closes people off from one another, and it is assumed that people in conversation over a cup of coffee are not 'working'. Much information is stored in computer systems but it is not organised effectively or maintained consistently, so it adds very little value to the organisation.

That is still too often the scenario we experience in today's organisations. We expect people to invest in their own skills and learning, yet we fail to develop the potential of one of the most powerful learning environments available – that of our own organisation. Just as a factory manager in the industrial age would be expected to provide workers with the production environment and necessary tools for the job, so knowledge-age leaders should provide their employees with the learning environment and knowledge tools to enable them to be effective. Research has shown that individual intelligence is measured by the density of connections in the brain. In the intelligent organisation of the future, every possible facility to connect people will be used. The leaders of intelligent organisations will know that this is not a fuzzy management fad – it's the licence for staying in business in the twenty-first century.

Andy Westwood is head of policy research at the Industrial Society. He joined the Industrial Society from the Employment Policy Institute. He has extensive experience and knowledge of both education and the labour market and has managed research projects with the Department for Education and Employment, the Prince's Trust, the Further Education Development Agency and the Economic and Social Research Council.

Andy worked as a lecturer and manager in further education for several years and was responsible for developing community and work-based learning projects. Andy works for the Department for Education and Employment on subjects including New Deal, the future of work and general employment policy. Andy also writes and comments for a range of broadcast and print media, including BBC TV and Radio News, the *New Statesman*, the *Guardian* and Sky.

3 | Drawing a line – who is going to train our workforce?

Andy Westwood

Governments and gurus agree: in today's post-industrial economy we are being forced to live increasingly through our knowledge and skills, as individuals, organisations, regions and nations. The existence of a knowledge economy may be as exaggerated as the growth of the high-performance workplace,[1] and yet there are significant, if not seismic, changes in our labour market and the way we work. Whatever the spin, it is clear that the work we do and the way we do it has changed.

Real change and the rhetoric of change both point to an increasing focus on education and training both in, and for, the workplace. The future of workplace learning appears fundamental to all 'knowledge-driven' scenarios. Very few commentators predict stability and even fewer expect our existing learning policy to be adequate in the years ahead. Somewhere in our complex labour market with more jobs and more types of job than ever before, we need to reconsider where responsibilities for learning should exist. It is this debate that will become the biggest single predictor of how workplace learning will change in the future. It will change our practices, policies and individual careers and it is vital that it does so. We have an underskilled, underproductive and underemployed workforce – we must 'learn' to improve.

Before we get too carried away, it is useful to consider some definitions in this minefield of mythologising and pedagogy. Principally we should agree with Helena Kennedy, who refers to the 'false dichotomy between education and training'.[2] These are not different sectors. They do not involve different approaches or techniques. They are the same. Those that argue otherwise are typically more motivated by myopic self-aggrandisement and business opportunity rather than workplace performance.

The best definition yet has been supplied by the Performance and Innovation Unit at the Cabinet Office in the introduction to its investigation into UK workforce development:

Workforce development is, broadly, the training and development employees (and potential employees) receive that is relevant to the workplace. This includes both on-the-job and off-the-job training, and can be recognised in formal qualifications, and in internal qualifications (which may or may not be accredited to external standards). Workforce development can include academic, subject-based training; but more typically covers more work-related, vocational training – from general communication, people and management skills to sector, industry and firm-specific skills.[3]

Learning both 'in' and 'for' the workplace, though, has to come under some scrutiny. How useful is learning in the workplace? How widespread? Who learns in the workplace? What do people learn? How can workplace learning specifically facilitate change in the workplace? What does the future hold for workplace learning?

Such scrutiny is not new. In 1776 Adam Smith suggested that 'the greater part of what is taught in schools and universities...does not seem to be the most proper preparation for business'.[4] At the introduction of the Elementary Education Act in 1870, W.E. Forster said: 'We must not delay. Upon the speedy provision of elementary education depends our industrial prosperity. It is no use trying to give technical teaching to our artisans without elementary education.' In more recent years the vocational system has continued to be the subject of political intervention. In 1976, the then Prime Minister, James Callaghan, said:

I am concerned on my journeys to find complaints from industry that new recruits from the schools sometimes do not have the basic tools to do the job that is required…there is concern about the standards of numeracy of school leavers...the basic purposes of education require the same essential tools. These are to be basically literate, to be basically numerate.[5]

The UK's vocational education and training system remains in crisis and out of touch with the changes in the labour market. There have been three important changes in the labour market in the last 30 years, and the system has failed to adequately react to each. Firstly and most obviously, there has been a major decline in the number of people in manual employment – the most notable aspect of manufacturing's decline in the UK. The share of skilled manual workers in total employment has fallen from 18 per cent to 12 per cent (there are currently 3.2 million such workers). Despite this shift, our learning systems are still too heavily influenced by the 'psyche' of manufacturing – apprenticeships, craft skills and 'technical' colleges.

Second, there has been a rise in skilled employment of people performing managerial, professional and technical jobs. The share of workers in these occupations has risen from a quarter to a third. The education and training world has been quick to exploit this shift. It has reacted disproportionately. MBAs, celebrity motivation seminars and leadership programmes compete successfully for training expenditure. Management colleges, universities, private training providers, not-for-profit institutes and even further education providers all contribute to this cash-rich overkill.

And third, there has been a rise in mixed but essentially low formal skilled employment performed by a group classified as 'personal and protective' workers. These jobs are most evident in the expansion of new shops and restaurants, and also in the growth of personal service occupations such as childcare. Their share of total employment has risen from around 6 per cent to around 11 per cent. The service sector generally does not seem to have an easy association with formal workplace learning. This is where assessments and systems have proved most cumbersome. Leading employers have subsequently withdrawn from nationally recognised schemes.[6]

There are two other parallel developments that have occurred behind these headline shifts. A kind of 'winner-takes-all' effect is seen within all occupations, with a widening pay gap between different groups of workers and also within different groups of workers. The increased use of technology in many workplaces, whichever sector they are in, has also had a huge, if slightly inconclusive, effect.

Both developments have made the future for workplace learning significantly worse. There is a very simple training divide in the UK between those who can access it and those who cannot. 'Winner-takes-all' economics has affected training budgets as much as salary bills.

'There is a very simple training divide in the UK between those who can access it and those who cannot.'

Access to workforce development is unequal, with managers and professionals or those with a degree up to five times more likely to receive work-based training than people with no qualification and/or in an unskilled job. E-learning may only make things worse. A simple Internet enquiry via any UK search engine will reveal a plethora of opportunities for managers. MBAs, management colleges and leadership dominate. It is significantly harder to find programmes for people lower down the ladder.

Table 1 | Exclusion from training over last five years (%)

Unskilled	71%
Partly skilled	68%
Skilled manual	51%
Skilled non-manual	48%
Managerial	26%
Professional	20%
No qualification	70%
CSE or equivalent	51%
O-Level	38%
A-Level	38%
Degree or above	24%

Source: Francis Green, University of Kent, 2000.

The future for learning in the UK workplace may be bleak. The present suggests that there is already a widening gap between those that have access to training opportunities and those that do not. In this sense the future scenario is one of a developing learning 'apartheid' facilitated by technology and distorted by the market.

Why do we care about the future of work-based learning?

Work-based learning is a big industry. Changes in the way we work increase interest in the future and in change-centred learning. The impact of technology is a constant question, as is the mismatch between our education system and the demand of employers – what Wendy Alexander, Scotland's Minister for Enterprise and Lifelong Learning, refers to as the 'blind date between training and the workplace'.[7] However, the real interest – politically at least – is in the link between work-based learning and productivity.

Productivity is firmly on the political agenda. Improving it will be a key objective in Labour's second term in government. The UK has consistently underperformed its major industrialised counterparts in Europe, North America and the Far East. In 1998, productivity[8] was 13 per cent higher in Germany than in the UK, 21 per cent higher in France and 36 per cent higher in the USA. The UK has as many graduates as France or Germany, but only half as many with intermediate level qualifications[9] as Germany and two-thirds of the number in France.

The Government's diagnosis of the problem is that underinvestment and underparticipation in work-based learning is the primary cause of our relatively poor levels of productivity. This conclusion is also shared by Adam Smith in his *Wealth of Nations*:

> The annual produce of the land and labour of any nation can be increased in its value by no other means but by increasing either the number of productive labourers, or the productive powers of those labourers who had before been employed.

Is this a fair conclusion? Not on the face of the evidence. Table 2 clearly shows that the UK workforce at least engages in work-related training.

Table 2 | Participation by adults aged 25–64 in continuing education and training by type of training and labour force status, 1994–1995 (%)

	All education and training	Job-related training
Australia	35.6	30.3
Belgium	21.6	14.0
Canada	36.5	29.5
Ireland	22.0	15.7
The Netherlands	36.3	24.1
New Zealand	46.4	38.4
Poland	14.0	10.6
Sweden	54.3	n/a
Switzerland	41.7	26.5
United Kingdom	**44.9**	**39.7**
United States	41.9	37.8
Unweighted Mean	***35.9***	***26.7***

Source: OECD (IALS), 1998.

Participation suggests, then, that this is not the problem. Nor does it seem that levels of employer investment are a problem either. The same OECD survey suggests that employers of all sizes invest comparatively high amounts in work-based learning in the UK. However, if we scratch below the surface and return to Francis Green's evidence, we can quickly see that this participation is dominated by those individuals in management positions or with high levels of previous learning. We can also assume therefore that the high levels of spending that are taking place are also at these levels. There is then a level of exclusion from work-based learning in terms of both participation and spending, which confirms the diagnosis that the UK suffers from a shortage of intermediate level skills.[10]

Even amongst the high participation groups we can see that this activity adds up to very small totals of actual training time. In terms of hours, the UK average for training hours per year is 99.5 hours per participating person. This is 35 hours below the OECD average and behind such countries as Ireland (218.7 hours per person per year), Holland (159 hours per person) and Poland (with 143 hours) – in fact, the UK total is behind all countries except the USA, which has an average of 98 hours per person.[11]

To summarise, we seem to spend a lot of money on training that doesn't last very long and on people who may not need it. Of course if we see training expenditure as part of a reward and retention strategy for UK managers, then there will be little reason to worry about a divided, market-led future. However, 'winner-takes-all' economics will not address the UK's productivity problem.

The future will be...?

The future requires a radical rethink of how we spend on work-based learning and who in the workforce we spend it on. Significant intervention from government will be necessary if we are to move the economy towards the knowledge-driven model that it craves. New lines will need to be drawn – and drawn quickly.

> ***'Significant intervention from government will be necessary if we are to move the economy towards the knowledge-driven model that it craves.'***

Higher government intervention – and spending – on behalf of lower earners, low-skilled and unskilled workers, transient workers, part-time workers and others on the fringes of the labour market will be necessary. These are typically the last groups of people that benefit from employer spending. Higher government intervention on behalf of small businesses will also be necessary if we are to address the existing inequalities in access to workforce development.

Government and businesses need to draw a new line – a line that will dominate the future of learning in the workplace. The Government can and should commit itself to a guarantee of basic transferable ability throughout the workforce. This should involve a universal entitlement to learning up to intermediate skill levels. Individual Learning Accounts and institutional funding, employer and union subsidies and any entitlement to study time should be concentrated here. This is not where employers should be exhorted to spend their money.

On the other side of the line, employers will have to reappraise their spending. Real work-based learning will inevitably cost more but will be more relevant to their bottom lines. Organisations will have to spend less on athletes and actors giving frothy motivational seminars to managers and more on real learning throughout their workforces. Technology will have to be harnessed appropriately – to efficiently spread learning throughout organisations and not just to be a new way of spending more on people at the top.

A new line will end Wendy Alexander's 'blind date', improve productivity and move the UK closer to a real 'knowledge economy'. It will bring government and employer priorities into the open. There will be nowhere to hide for the mythologists of management, training and, more lately, e-learning. It will be a simple future with simple responsibilities.

Endnotes

1. See the work of SKOPE – Ewart Keep and Ken Mayhew (www.economics.ox.ac.uk/SKOPE/).
2. Speech to the Adam Smith Institute at No. 11 Downing Street, 1998.
3. Performance and Innovation Unit Cabinet Office website, 2000 (www.cabinet.office.gov.uk/innovation/home/homef.html).
4. *Inquiry into the Nature and Causes of the Wealth of Nations*, 1776.
5. Ruskin College speech, 1976.
6. Tesco withdrew from offering NVQs and its accelerated graduate recruitment scheme in the late1990s.
7. In a speech to the Industrial Society and the Economic and Social Research Council, March 2001.
8. As measured by output per worker.
9. Equivalent to NVQ Levels II and III.
10. See the reports of the National Skills Task Force (www.skillsbase.dfee.gov.uk/default.asp).
11. Average duration of training undertaken by employed adults aged 25–64 in continuing education and training by type of training, 1994–1995. Source: OECD, 1998.

Ewart Keep has a BA in modern history and politics (London University) and a PhD in industrial relations (Warwick University). Between first degree and doctorate he worked for the CBI's Education, Training and Technology Directorate. Since 1985 he has been employed at the University of Warwick, firstly in the Industrial Relations Research Unit (IRRU), and, since 1998, as deputy director of a new Economic and Social Research Council (ESRC) centre on Skills, Knowledge and Organisational Performance (SKOPE). Keep was a member of the DfEE Skills Task Force Research Group, and has published extensively on UK vocational education and training policy, work-based learning for the young, the links between skills and competitive strategies, and the learning society and the learning organisation. In 2000 he authored the Centre for Scottish Public Policy's new horizon report, *Upskilling Scotland*. He has undertaken work for the European Commission, the CIPD, DfEE and Scottish Enterprise, and is currently acting as an advisor to the Cabinet Office Performance and Innovation Unit's project on workforce development.

4 | The skills system in 2015

Ewart Keep

Introduction

In 2015 the national skills system, particularly as it focuses upon the needs of the workplace, bears little if any resemblance to the jumble of traditional skills supply initiatives that were still around when the new century dawned. The concept of what a training policy should be concerned with has shifted dramatically, as have the ways in which policies are made and then delivered. Why did this change take place?

The reasons for the new approach

These were essentially two-fold. First, by the early 2000s it was becoming increasingly obvious that, although the target of a blizzard of initiatives and near-ceaseless institutional change, these were not producing the desired result. These schemes had included:

- Individual Learning Accounts (ILAs)
- Graduate Apprenticeships
- Foundation Modern Apprenticeships (FMAs)
- Employer Transferable Training Loans
- Employer Learning Network Fund
- People Skill Scoreboards
- National Adult Basic Skills Strategy
- Union Learning Fund
- Adult and Community Learning Fund.

Overall, it was clear that government skills and training policies were failing to deliver lasting and significant change on a number of fronts. For example:

- The qualification system remained a sprawling, complex mess, incomprehensible to employers and trainees alike.
- Despite several waves of reorganisation and reform, in many parts of the economy sectoral training organisations remained weak, ineffective and unable to bring to bear very much purchase on the decision-making of their members.

'...it was clear that government skills and training policies were failing to deliver lasting and significant change on a number of fronts.'

- The problem of securing an effective, high-quality work-based route for the initial vocational education and training of young entrants to the labour force remained unresolved. In some sectors and firms, modern apprenticeships had been a great success, but in many others the quality of the learning experiences remained low, as did completion rates.

- There continued to be significant segments of the adult workforce, particularly those in lower-status occupations, who received little if any training, particularly in the type of transferable skills that might enhance their employability in a rapidly changing labour market.

The fact that many of these problems had been around since the early 1980s and had defied solution led policy-makers to the conclusion that there were limits to what a traditionally framed skills policy and training system could achieve. Increasing the supply of skills, often through expansion of the education system, was a necessary but not sufficient condition for moving towards a higher-skilled economy. Perhaps a different policy approach, which encompassed wider changes, might be required to tackle these 'wicked' problems.

The second reason for a radical change of direction was the realisation that, at a broader level, there was a range of issues bound up with economic performance and social inclusion that had to be tackled if the country was to compete effectively and maintain cohesion as a society. Some of these centred on the persistence of a productivity gap between all parts of the UK and many of our leading competitors, with environmental sustainability, and with the very slow and limited take-up of models of high-performance work organisation.

There was also concern that, in some sectors, a combination of technology, delivery systems and shifting consumer preferences was leading to 'commodification', whereby the good or service became increasingly sold almost exclusively on the basis of price (the most frequently cited examples were air travel and insurance). Other worries centred on the dangers of a labour market in which there were some signs of polarisation, and where income inequality was continuing to grow. There was also evidence that the limited demands being placed on workers by many jobs undermined attempts to renew and sustain basic skills among the adult workforce.

Overall, there was a realisation that, if things were simply left to chance or the working through of market forces, not enough organisations were likely to 'raise their game' in terms of product and service quality, people management systems or training. The result would be a failure to develop the kind of economy and working environment that society demanded.

The dimensions of the new approach

The good thing about repeated failure is that, sooner or later, it generally leads to a reappraisal. If the failure is widespread, the reappraisal may need to be radical. In this case it was.

Joined-up policy thinking and a joined-up vision

Given the range and nature of the issues that needed to be addressed, it was clear that they could not be tackled by skills policies alone: skills had to become integrated into a wider and more co-ordinated attempt at systemic reform. This reform agenda drew together various inherently related strands of policy and activity, such as:

- attempt to raise productivity
- boost research and development spend and innovation
- continue to attract inward investment
- manage rises in the national minimum wage
- promote social inclusion and cohesion
- regenerate severely deprived areas
- adapt to the challenges of an ageing workforce.

More fundamentally, the Government, in conjunction with many other partners and stakeholders, evolved a long-term vision of where the country should be heading. This vision encompassed:

- a high-wage, high-productivity economy, where all shared in the country's success
- an internationally competitive economy, with a strong export sector, and with an increasing proportion of organisations producing higher-value-added goods and services
- a country with a vibrant culture, capable of maintaining its own identity in a globalised world
- a country with strong notions of citizenship and with empowered individuals, organisations, communities, localities and regions, willing and able to play an active part in shaping their own social, economic and political destinies
- a tolerant, just and inclusive society
- a country that is an attractive place to live.

Each of these was an ambitious goal in its own right. Taken together, they represented an agenda for radical change, and the long-term policy implications of this vision are still being played out.

Skills and what else to make the difference?

This new approach meant the end to free-standing policies that saw skills and training as a magic bullet that could, on its own, transform economic performance or deliver social inclusion. Instead, skills policies have come to nest within and support broader policy goals, and to be promoted and delivered accordingly.

In the economic sphere the overarching vision has meant concerted attempts to encourage and support more organisations to shift towards the production of higher-value-added goods and services. Business strategy has become the prime focus for policy. A range of instruments is being applied, including consumer education to create a more demanding market, public purchasing policies that aim to ratchet up quality in those organisations that seek to supply public services or sell to the public sector, and anti-poverty measures to help increase the segment of the domestic market who are not forced to buy exclusively on the basis of price. Simultaneously, there have been major efforts to shift productivity levels upwards.

'...the skills supply and enhancement policies of 2015 operate within...wider efforts...to improve competitive strategies, HRM policies, work organisation and job design.'

Having made clear where they think the economy should be heading, government (national, regional and local) has been revolutionising business support services in order to offer help to organisations seeking to make this transition. One key element of this support is advice and subsidised consultancy services to aid organisations, particularly SMEs that lack their own well-developed HR function, to think through and deliver work reorganisation and job redesign that can improve productivity and sustain higher-quality competitive strategies. A central component is the promotion of high-performance/high-involvement models of people management. Naturally, these changes bring with them demands for new and better skills, and work reorganisation can also help many employees put to better and more productive use the skills and knowledge they already possess. Public-sector workplaces have an important part in this process, acting as test beds for innovation and the trial of new methods of work organisation and learning, and as exemplars of good practice. The Government has rediscovered the value of leading by example.

Overall, in contrast to traditional skills initiatives, the skills supply and enhancement policies of 2015 operate within, and as an integral part of, wider efforts to encourage firms to improve their competitive strategies, HRM policies, work organisation and job design. Instead of simply trying to increase the supply of skills and assuming that this will, of itself, be enough to produce thoroughgoing change at a strategic level, skills initiatives now take their strength from being part of a much broader approach. Upskilling has become a need that is derived from organisational and strategic changes rather than the main driver of such change. More and better training is sold on the back of wider developments.

This shift in focus has helped to raise the profile of skills issues within organisations, as it has ceased to become a bolt-on activity and become one of the prime foundations for supporting organisational transformation. It has also helped remove the tendency to oversell the impact that any training intervention can be expected to have. By integrating skills into business strategy, people now understand much better where skills fit into the overall picture and what they can be expected to deliver and why.

The new system

A joined-up strategy requires joined-up institutions, and the training infrastructure serves two overarching organisations. The prime body is the Competitiveness Board, which is made up of representatives from the relevant national government departments covering trade and industry, working life issues and education; regional government; and a range of stakeholders, such as business support organisations, employer bodies, the CIPD and social partners. The other organisation with oversight in this field is the Social Inclusion and Citizenship Board, which commissions and funds skill interventions that support equality and social inclusiveness agendas. The two boards work closely together.

Beneath these two bodies are the various national and regional government departments and the many different institutions and networks that deliver skills. These include inter-firm networks within industrial clusters, local group associations, sectoral bodies, local colleges, private training providers and individual employers.

Policy-making is now conducted by project teams, made up of civil servants (from national, regional and local government), practitioners and academic experts. The involvement of those who have to implement the initiative in framing its design has helped to reduce the likelihood of resistance to and failure of policy interventions. Governmental skills in the field of change management have undergone a sea change.

The emphasis of spending has shifted from that of earlier times. Rather than concentrate on just the volume of throughput, a far higher proportion of public money is invested in developing and maintaining systemic capacity in the business support and training systems. For example, sectoral bodies are resourced at a level that allows them to play a significant and comprehensive role in both forecasting and securing the skills needed for their industry. Capacity-building embraces substantial efforts to improve the training of trainers and the development of mentoring, people management and work organisation/job design skills in the general managerial workforce.

There is a network of research centres (one run by the CIPD) that undertake labour market research as well as theoretical and applied research, including action research and developmental projects in the field of skills and workplace learning. One of the areas where such centres have had the greatest impact is in furthering the understanding of, and capacity to use, the many forms of informal, on-the-job learning, so that such activity is embedded in day-to-day management of the workplace. The systematic use of such techniques as mentoring, job rotation, project work, and expert networks has spread at a fast pace. E-learning and the capacity of IT to facilitate communication and record learning events have helped.

The relationship between education and training has also been refined. After much, often heated, debate employers are clear what they can expect in terms of skills and knowledge from those leaving the education system. They are also clear where their responsibilities for socialising new entrants into the workplace begin. The principle of establishing clear rights, responsibilities and duties has been used throughout the education and training system. The clarity that this has brought has been an unambiguous good.

The way in which the system is managed has also undergone dramatic change. The tendency prevalent in the 1990s and early 2000s of trying to manage everything through externally imposed targets (a very primitive form of management by objective) has largely been abandoned. The tendency for such targets to produce unforeseen perverse incentives and to warp the balance of activities became increasingly apparent. Instead, there have been real efforts to move towards a more high-trust system, where regional, local, social partnership and sectoral bodies are expected to set their own performance goals, where necessary with support and advice from the national boards.

The impact on organisations

The increasing emphasis upon the adoption of the high-performance workplace model, coupled with the better integration of skills issues into strategic planning, have had a profound impact on organisations. The status of those who deal with personnel issues has risen, as has the salience of their potential role in the formulation of organisational strategy. The advice and support of expert trainers in devising and helping embed new learning opportunities within work have been crucial, and a great deal of money and effort has been invested in the long-neglected area of the training of trainers.

At the same time, the demands posed by the high-performance model have raised the importance of people management skills to the whole of the management population. Management training and appraisal and reward systems now all place a heavy emphasis upon this area of managerial activity. Indeed, as the shift towards more high-performance working took off, it was soon recognised that perhaps the largest skill requirement it generated related to the managers who had to implement and sustain this change in their workplaces. Very often the persistence of old-fashioned management styles and strategies was found to result from the narrowness and weakness of managerial skills and an inability to do anything other than what had always been done. Breaking this 'path dependence' has taken much time and effort, but it has been one of the keys to success.

The state of play

It would be wrong to portray these changes as having been easy. They have not been. The new policies have required profound shifts in the roles of different actors and a new style of policy formation that many have found uncomfortable, at least to begin with.

There have also been some serious tensions between what society and government aspire to and what organisations have been willing and able to do – not least in terms of accommodating a shift from the short- to the long-term as the right horizon for performance (and profit) measurement.

The important thing is that policy and practice are now grounded in a new understanding of where skills fit into the wider picture of competitiveness and social inclusion. This more holistic approach marks a decisive break with the past, and one upon which it seems unlikely there will be any going back.

Charles Leadbeater is an independent writer and an adviser to leading companies. He studied politics, philosophy and economics at Balliol College, Oxford, before becoming a journalist. Charles is a senior research associate with the independent think-tank Demos, and has written reports and pamphlets on social and civic entrepreneurship and on cultural and knowledge entrepreneurs. He is an adviser to the Downing Street Policy Unit and the DTI, and has drafted government White Papers on competitiveness and communication. He also advised the European Commission, working as a special adviser on competitiveness and the new economy in the run-up to the EU's Lisbon summit in spring 2000.

Charles writes a regular column for the *Industry Standard* magazine as well as contributing regularly to the *New Statesman*, *Business and Strategy* and the *Financial Times*. He spent 10 years working on the *Financial Times* and later worked on the *Independent*. His most recent book, *Living on Thin Air: The new economy*, was published in the UK in 1999.

5 | Learning and work – authorship

Charles Leadbeater

Innovation

Innovation, intangibles, information and intelligence are the driving forces for the modern economy. These forces also frame the future of work and the role that learning will play in preparing people for work.

Innovation is at the heart of our society's cult of change. We invest systematically in change – through research, development and innovation – to develop new ideas and turn them into new products more quickly than ever before and then to spread these products around the world more quickly. We live in a culture constantly in transition, on the way to somewhere else. The next upgrade is always just around the corner.

In contrast, even a century ago research and development was often rudimentary within companies. New ideas often arrived not by design but by chance. Fashions were confined to those who could afford such frivolity; they did not sweep the entire society.

The centrality of innovation, the constant search for the new, explains the significance of the other three 'I's of the modern economy. We live in an increasingly intangible economy, in which assets that cannot be weighed or shipped in railway cars – brands, ideas, software, relationships – deliver more value. The spread of information and communications networks means that new ideas and products travel faster than ever before to larger markets. Chief among those corporate assets is the combined intelligence and imagination of people who work for a company. Companies increasingly rest on their ability to excite and combine the intelligence and ideas of the people who work for them, to devise new products and services.

'Companies increasingly rest on their ability to excite and combine the intelligence and ideas of the people who work for them, to devise new products and services.'

This innovation-driven economy spreads alarm as well as offering great promise of a better future. More rapid and discontinuous change means more upheaval and instability. For those in work that will mean more transitions between technologies, working practices, occupations and organisations. Many will find those transitions painful and unsettling. Capacities to cope with change – financial resources, inner confidence, the ability to sense new opportunities and learn new ways of earning a living – are not evenly spread. There are many places in the UK – places with skills and cultures of work that grew up around large employers in manufacturing – where people are completely cut off from the new economy. They are marooned.

This increasingly knowledge-driven economy will deliver quite different experiences of work for different people. It may spawn a liberated new generation of free agents, skilled independent knowledge workers who are confident enough to demand decent rewards for their intellectual capital. But, equally, new technologies will allow more surveillance of service workers, 24–7. The boundaries between home and office are blurring for many professionals. That can both mean liberating flexibility or unwarranted intrusion. The new economy is creating a hyper-mobile, cosmopolitan workforce of highly skilled professionals. But at the same time there is evidence that more service jobs and micro-companies are working within local economies of tourism, retailing, leisure and entertainment.

The new world of work

The new world of work will mean quite different things to people with different skills, backgrounds and social networks. As a result it is hard to find common themes to the character of work that a comprehensive education and learning system should prepare everyone for. Nevertheless, several candidates suggest themselves.

One candidate for a generic capability all people will need is creativity: to find and solve problems facing customers, for example. As innovation becomes more important, so should a capacity for creativity. Perhaps creativity should be at the heart of learning for the new economy – except that the reality is quite a lot of work will not be that creative, although it may well require a high level of skills and initiative. Creative people are often seen as slightly deviant. Globalisation, competition and relentless pressures from financial markets mean that companies will not tolerate deviations from very demanding standards for performance and quality. As much as we might like to imagine that work will be more creative, it will also require meticulous attention to detail and quality.

Technology skills are another natural candidate, given that more jobs will require knowledge of computers and communications. But most young people seem quite at home with computers. Indeed many learn so much under their own steam, often at home, that they find information technology lessons at school a bore. Many future jobs will be in human and personal services: education, healthcare, domestic services. Rather than promote yet more learning for technology in computer classes, perhaps we should invest in the arts, drama, music and sport, to develop human capacities for empathy, understanding and care.

In an economy driven by the generation, acquisition, application and exploitation of distinctive know-how, it would make sense to prepare people for work by making sure they study to a high level in some specialist areas, to build up a core of knowledge in maths and sciences, for example. There is ample evidence that the British economy has been held back by a lack of research and technical skills in industry. Yet as education improves in quality and more of the population gain degrees and professional qualifications, there is a danger that we will enter a period of qualification inflation: skills and capabilities that cannot be taught, commodified or standardised because they are based on tacit knowledge or lessons learned from experience. Rather than encourage people to undergo more formal education before work, by starting school earlier and making formal education last longer, perhaps we should be encouraging young people to learn more outside school, to acquire the distinctive experiences and views on life that will really matter.

The concept of authorship

Amid all these conflicting and confusing tendencies, however, at least one theme does stand out. We should prepare all people to claim authorship of their work. First, let me explain what this capacity for 'authorship' means before examining why it matters so much and how people can learn to acquire it.

The idea of authorship overlaps with many of the other ideas that swirl around the future of work: creativity, empowerment, self-employment and self-management. What is distinctive about authorship and what does it add?

'The value of authorship applies not just to a single job but to how people weave together careers in the modern labour market.'

Authorship means creating something that embodies your voice, your distinctive view of the world and the set of experiences that you bring to work. To see work as a process of authorship is to see it as a form of self-expression, not a task imposed upon you from the outside. When people are authors of their work, they feel they shape it, own it. The craft that authors apply to their work gives them a sense of satisfaction and achievement. Work involving authorship cannot be managed well through detailed attention to process and yardsticks. Providing people with a sense that they are authors of their own work means managing by outcome and deadline rather than by process.

The value of authorship applies not just to a single job but to how people weave together careers in the modern labour market. Increasingly people are authors of their own careers, putting together the mix of training, assignments and time off from work that best meets their aspirations. Thirty years ago more people might have seen their future working life as fitting themselves into a career template in a profession, trade or community. These days we want to be authors of our own career trajectories and of the way we work.

This culture of independent self-management that allows people to see themselves reflected in their work is increasingly central not just to so-called 'knowledge worker' jobs, for example in the professions, advertising and design, but also to front-line service jobs. In a world of automated call centres and electronic customer relationship management, customers will increasingly value human and social contact: staff who can take the time to understand and then respond to particular customer needs rather than sticking to a crib sheet.

So the key capability that people must learn to acquire is how to exert a sense of authorship of their work and careers. Why does this sense of authorship matter so much, both for employees and employers, workers and customers?

For many people cut off by change, left behind in communities created around manufacturing industries, access to work is still the critical issue. A hum-drum job in a call centre with precious little sense of authorship is still better than no job. However, even in these front-line jobs initiative, problem-solving and character will come to play a more important role, and the people who enter the job market in these 'service factory' jobs will only move on by claiming a sense of authorship of their work.

Anxiety is a problem for many people in work, worried about the security of their jobs or how they combine being a parent with being a committed and ambitious employee. Yet these people yearn for a sense of authorship, a sense that their jobs and careers are under their control rather than subject to the whim of markets or the demands of senior managers.

Perhaps the most profound problem afflicting modern work is neither access nor anxiety but, to use a rather unfashionable word, a deep sense of alienation: the feeling that your work is not your own, that it does not belong to you and does not reflect your values, desires and aspirations. This sense of alienation is at the heart of the central paradox that companies, especially large companies, face in their approach to work.

Authorship at work

The global, always on, 24–7, financially driven market demands that work is highly organised and target-driven. Nothing can be left to chance. All costs have to be justified. No deviation from demanding standards for quality and productivity will be tolerated. Yet the growing need to compete through innovation and branding implies that work needs to be an open and creative process to which people must feel personally committed. The 24–7 work culture, in which people never feel their time is quite their own, leads to a quiet withdrawal, a sense of reluctance or caution on the part of employees, which means they are less willing to engage in the kind of highly committed, creative work needed to drive innovation. The way out of this trap, both for companies and employees, is to encourage a sense of authorship at work.

For workers, the idea of authorship of work will become far more important as companies seek to appeal to successive generations brought up to value and articulate their sense of independence. This generation will also have more opportunities, through self-employment, extended study and micro-entrepreneurship, to pursue this sense of independence if employers do not provide it.

The creativity and innovation demanded by the modern economy are impossible without work becoming more about self-expression. Creativity is partly a product of technical, problem-solving skills. But it also often requires a degree of emotional commitment lacking at work.

Entrepreneurship, the ability to sense opportunities and mobilise resources to exploit them, will become increasingly important in large and small companies. That capacity to sense an opportunity and articulate it confidently and compellingly often comes from having a distinctive view of the world. Entrepreneurs have a strong sense of authorship: they give voice to their ambitions through the kinds of company they build.

In a world in which people are likely to have more than one career, more than one period as an adult in study or education and several different kinds of employment contract, it will be increasingly difficult for them to make sense of where their work life is headed by reference to external yardsticks. When I started work almost 20 years ago there was a kind of template that budding journalists had to follow that provided some shape to their career. That has long gone. These days people need a much stronger inner sense of direction and purpose to shape their work amidst much greater fluidity.

It is not just that authorship makes sense for those at work: it also makes sense for employers. Companies that want to innovate more rapidly and respond to change more quickly need a motivated, self-aware, self-managing workforce. It is difficult for a company to claim to be the author of its own future if the individual people within it do not.

The growing tendency for products and services to be bundled together will put a premium on authored work. Take a manufacturing company such as Electrolux. When it simply made boxes for people to use at home, it could focus on efficiency and quality. It still has to, of course. But these days Electrolux sees itself as providing people with complete solutions to their domestic needs. It wants the purchase of an Electrolux product to kick off a service relationship between customer and company. Servicing these demands requires more than timeliness and efficiency. It means having a much more engaged, personalised and human approach to work. Customers are no longer numbers, but are people with problems.

However, the beauty of authored work is that it can also be highly efficient. Companies with a thin senior management hierarchy increasingly need to promote a culture of self-management at work, in which people around an organisation can be trusted to get on with their work, meet their targets and deliver their results without constant interference and intervention. The most efficient organisations are those where people understand what they need to do, want to do it and are armed with the right information and incentives to get on with the job without being told to do so. Authorship and self-management are the keys not just to creativity but also, in the long run, to reduced bureaucracy and improved efficiency.

We live in a world in which companies cannot afford to have their costs and quality far out of line with competition, often global competition. Yet we also live in a world in which innovation and creativity matter so much that companies cannot afford to have a workforce that is disloyal, disengaged and alienated. In the long run, companies will only square this circle by creating a sense of authorship at work, so that people can see themselves reflected in their work, rather than the demands of the forces of alienation – 'global capitalism', 'the system' or 'senior management'.

'Learning at school should increasingly teach children to sense opportunity and to seek and solve problems.'

Teaching authorship

How could people learn to acquire this sense of authorship? If claiming authorship over your working life is vital, then how might school, college and learning beyond the classroom prepare people better to claim it for themselves?

Authorship, like creativity, is a capacity that is very difficult to promote evenly. The British education system still struggles to deliver more quantifiable skills – literacy and numeracy – across all of society. So the chances of its delivering something as complex and intangible as a 'sense of authorship' are probably quite limited. Athough a sense of authorship may be developed and learned, it has to come from within. It cannot be taught and delivered from without. And it takes time, trial, error and experimentation, as much in the 'real world' of work as in the classroom. Learning about yourself, what you really want to do and what you are good at probably never ends. Learning does not prepare people for work so much as provide an essential ingredient of work.

However, even with those caveats in mind, the learning that people do before they start work can play an important role in making them more able to develop a sense of authorship. Learning at school should increasingly teach children to sense opportunity and to seek and solve problems. They should learn how to borrow ideas from other disciplines and people to augment their own.

As well as going to careers advisers, children need to be encouraged to become more able to understand and assess their own strengths and weaknesses. The more that work depends on a sense of inner direction, the more important it will be for people to be able to reach down inside themselves to understand what makes them tick.

Both the liberal arts and science will play a role in encouraging this sense of inquiry and self-expression. Learning needs to deliver a new mix of specialisation and breadth. Specialisation at later stages of schooling should reflect the ambitions and aspirations of children. But they should be expected to study a range of subjects organised around this special interest, because increasingly all careers will depend on being able to marshal knowledge from different disciplines.

Perhaps above all education and learning need to inculcate a spirit of self-management. We assess children primarily on their ability to understand and follow instructions, to take and carry out orders, to deliver on tasks set for them. Increasingly we will need to assess them on the tasks they set for themselves, their ability to find and solve problems that motivate them and how well they manage their own work.

We will only deliver that shift in the culture of learning with very far-reaching changes in the way that schools and colleges are organised. The best already know how to excite a sense of personal commitment from students within a framework of study set for them. The best schools encourage students to set demanding targets for themselves. They combine a clear sense of order and discipline, with the engine of self-motivation and self-expression.

So what about the future?

Three fundamental changes stand out.

First, education will have to become more personalised to reflect the ambitions and motivations of children. We have to teach children from an early age to take responsibility for their own motivation and drive. We can only do that if they see something vital in their education, to their sense of self and sense of achievement.

Second, we need to promote a culture of self-management in learning, so that children increasingly, as they get older, self-manage their work, set their targets and are assessed by not just what they produce to order but what they come up with themselves.

Third, that kind of learning needs to extend beyond the classroom. Kids learn at home, at play, in sport and drama. Learning to become the author of your own work can take place anywhere. Indeed, as schools are currently organised, the place it is least likely to happen is in the classroom.

Martyn Sloman was appointed to his current position as adviser, training and development at the CIPD in January 2001. From 1997–2000 he worked as director of management education and training for Ernst & Young, one of the largest business advisory firms in the world.

As author, lecturer and conference speaker he has contributed to the development of modern human resource concepts and practice. His new book, *The E-Learning Revolution*, was published by the CIPD in April 2001 and presents 21 separate propositions that will shape the introduction of e-learning. His earlier best-selling book, *A Handbook for Training Strategy* (Gower 1994), received wide critical acclaim and has now been reprinted, translated into Polish and Chinese and published in India. A second edition appeared in autumn 1999.

Martyn is an honorary teaching fellow in the Department of Organizational Psychology, Birkbeck College, University of London, and an industrial fellow at Kingston Business School.

6 | Sharing the power of learning

Martyn Sloman

Let's start with some uncontroversial statements. First, learning at work is a good thing for the individual learner, for the organisation concerned and for the economy as a whole. Second, learning will undergo a significant change as the potential of new technology is realised. The challenge is to manage, shape and realise this transition. The objective of more effective and more widespread learning will require the development of a shared agenda. This agenda must be implemented through the combined efforts of all involved in promoting learning at work.

My premise is that our best chances of success lie in harnessing the strong economic and personal drivers that motivate individuals to learn and organisations to provide them with the opportunities. Those who think that effective learning at work matters should be honest with each other, should make information available and should collaborate across boundaries. Moreover, a new model showing how this could be done has emerged as a result of developments in software.

This central premise is first developed through four short sections, which argue in turn that:

- learning is rather special
- effective interventions to promote learning are those that are valued by the individual and the organisation
- current patterns and structures will be placed under severe strain with the arrival of e-learning
- boundaries deter: institutions can create confusion.

Once this part of the argument is completed, the new model from software development – the open-source movement – is discussed and its relevance assessed. What can those of us who are committed to more effective learning draw from this approach? How can the lessons of open source be applied to learning at work?

> ***'...our best chances of success lie in harnessing the strong economic and personal drivers that motivate individuals to learn and organisations to provide them with the opportunities.'***

Why does learning at work matter?

Every reader of this publication is likely to have received at least some training in the workplace.[1] Many readers will have themselves delivered training or managed its delivery. Everyone will have their own view on why learning at work matters.

Successive governments, irrespective of political persuasion, have seen learning, development and training as drivers of business success and hence national prosperity. To quote from a mid-1990s government-sponsored publication:

> Training is seen as a key component in achieving empowerment of the individual and in maintaining focus on the customer in order to remain competitive. Not only is 'training the epicentre of empowerment' with as much as 10% of employees' time spent on it, but 'successful companies use education as a competitive weapon'.[2]

So a better-trained workforce will allow the UK to compete more effectively and to operate in higher-value markets. There is much to commend this sort of 'Let's all be like Manchester United' argument; the most damaging thing that can be said about it is that it has not achieved its aim. So far the new basis of competition has not led to across-the-board acceptance of workforce development and a greater commitment to training.

There are many reasons for this. The CIPD is putting considerable research effort into identifying the nature of the link between (on the one hand) effective people management and development and (on the other) economic performance. Such research could, hopefully, remove one of the main barriers to understanding and lead to the development of effective templates for practical action.

What must be evident by now, however, is that 'exhortative voluntarism' in itself has a limited effect. This can be defined as the attempt to describe and promote best practice in the hope that it is accepted and becomes adopted as universal reality.

An alternative to exhortative voluntarism is to build on the widespread goodwill that many of us feel towards learning. For those who hold this view, training and education are rather special goods and interventions. The acquisition of job-related skills gives people pride in their work: they can acquire new assurance and self-respect. They can build on this assurance to seek and acquire new capabilities. They can confront and overcome the challenge of economic change. We have all, for example, experienced the professionalism of the health service ward, or the pride taken in good personal service underpinned by training. It would be tragic if we lost sight of this personal and ethical dimension to learning at work in the wider economic debate.

What is an effective intervention?

The next step in the argument may seem so obvious as to amount to a tautology: effective training interventions are those that are valued by the individual and the organisation. What this means is that if something really matters (whether to the organisation or the individual), efforts will be made to make sure it happens. Such interventions will happen irrespective of institutional intervention from government – which could indeed detract rather than assist.

Some illustrations may assist.

Until recently I held a senior position in training and development at a large and successful business advisory firm. Time pressures were intensive and training events were always reduced to the bare minimum. Yet if a particular sort of technical, business or skills updating was required for a compelling business reason, it received immediate support. In these instances the organisation would move quickly and with commitment at all levels. A training intervention was judged to be important not in some abstract sense but because of its immediate impact on the way in which the firm competed.

The second illustration concerns my external teaching at Birkbeck College – one of the two institutions in the UK that have no full-time undergraduate students (the other is the Open University). I am astonished by the commitment of the students who often attend three evening lectures or seminars a week over a four-year period. Some of them are women with full-time jobs and small children. They are making this sacrifice to gain a university degree, which is a qualification with currency in the employment marketplace. A Birkbeck degree will help them get a better job.

The third illustration is a negative one that shows how we can fail to capture these motivational drivers. In the mid-1980s, as a management consultant, I undertook some work on management qualifications for the government training arm (then called the Manpower Services Commission). It became evident that there was a powerful demand for a three-tier level of management qualifications. This required the consolidation of a certificate and of a diploma in management to underpin the MBA, which was growing in terms of currency. This consolidation has not happened: it became lost in general institutional problems surrounding National Vocational Qualifications.

Others will doubtless have different views, but the underlying point is straightforward. There are many occasions where organisations and individuals exhibit considerable energy towards learning and training. The task is to harness that energy. Fortunately, changing technology offers us a new opportunity.

The arrival of e-learning

Much has been written about the potential impact of e-learning. In truth, we don't know how it will develop, and we must recognise there are a whole number of critical questions to be addressed on its implementation. What cannot be denied, however, is its potential.

We have acquired the ability to deliver up-to-date information from internal and external sources to an individual learner at his or her desk. The American Society for Training and Development uses the following quotation from the science fiction writer William Gibson to illustrate the power of the transition: 'The future's already arrived; it's just not evenly distributed yet.'

Leading-edge organisations, particularly in the USA, are pushing the envelope and implementing some exciting new approaches to the delivery of training. Not every organisation will be a best-practice organisation, but a reasonable prediction of the future for e-learning will run as follows. There will be a shift away from classroom training, affecting how training is delivered and the way people will learn; the corporate intranet will become the most important vehicle for delivery; about a quarter of training in organisations will be delivered using learning technology.

'...power will shift from producers to consumers (the learner being the ultimate consumer).'

Current actors in training (learners, corporate trainers, external providers, educational institutions etc) will be affected in different ways. The structure and disposition of the industry evolved before the emergence of the Internet and e-learning. It will be placed under some strain. Information will become more widely available and transparent: experiences can be communicated and shared. In general, power will shift from producers to consumers (the learner being the ultimate consumer).

We will need to develop a new vocabulary and think in terms of supply or value chains (the system that links together the forward flow of materials to the customer and the backward flow of information from customer to producers and intermediaries). Any part of the supply chain that does not add value will disappear in time, and relationships along that chain will change.

There are huge opportunities here, and we can expect some powerful interventions in the market. In April 2001, for example, the Massachusetts Institute of Technology (MIT) announced its plans to make the material for nearly all of its courses freely available over the Internet over the next 10 years. MIT described this as an unprecedented step in worldwide education to challenge the privatisation of knowledge. One can only respect and admire such intentions and hope that it is a harbinger of the future. In contrast, a press release a fortnight later announcing agreement between a well-known software company and a training provider deserves a more cynical response: they announced that they'd joined forces to 'train a nation'. It is not known whether the Government has accepted this offer.

Can institutions cope?

The arrival of e-learning is a disruptive force. Changes in supply chains are inevitable and will increasingly take place in a global context. Given this background, it is fair to ask if government organisations and educational institutions can adapt sufficiently rapidly to meet the challenge of change. Time alone will tell. Some nimble footwork will be required from educational institutions that are not noted for their ability to move quickly. There are two real dangers here: first, an ineffective infrastructure could slow down the pace of change and suppress the powerful motivational forces that drive effective learning and, second, a profusion of intermediaries could cause confusion and negate the very transparency that should work to the benefit of the learner.

Certainly there does appear to be a proliferation of government-sponsored organisations involved in promoting learning. The newly created Learning and Skills Councils will, we are led to understand, work with the National Learning and Skills Council, the DfEE, Regional Developmental Agencies, the Employment Services (and its agencies), local authorities, the National Training Organisations network, the small business service, Connexions, learndirect, the adult learning inspectorate and OFSTED. This list does not, of course, include local colleges or voluntary bodies. Again, I must draw on my personal experience. Since taking up my current role I have been amazed at the number of bodies – all with acronyms or abbreviations, all very worthy – that seek a role in promoting or managing the learning experience. At a time of disruptive change they will be threatened and will seek to justify that role. It would be tragic if the energy that should be put into assisting learners to grasp new opportunities is devoted to the concerns of organisational chauvinism. In short, if organisations and intermediaries do not adapt they will act as barriers to effective learning.

What can we learn from open source?

The emergence of e-learning, then, will unleash powerful forces. The market for the provision of training will become more transparent and hence more efficient. Institutions will have to adapt. The creation of new institutions by government is of questionable value at this stage. There is, however, a new opportunity here to harness and reinforce the strong personal and organisational drivers that lead to effective learning at work and elsewhere. Moreover, there is another possible dimension that could come into force: that of the community. A consideration of the open-source movement in software gives an indication of what could be.

The open-source movement is a collection of software programmers who are committed to working together in a particular way. Open source depends on the willingness and ability of programmers freely to share their source code (the basic building block of programming) so that others can improve it. To quote from the opensource.org website:

> When programmers on the Internet can read, redistribute and modify the source for a piece of software, it evolves. People improve it, people adapt it, and people fix bugs. And this can happen at a speed that, if one is used to the slow pace of conventional software, seems astonishing.[3]

In short, this sharing of information and collaborative building produces better software than what can be described as the closed model.

Open-source methods have produced many successful programmes: the most prominent is the widely used Linux operating system. The open-source movement is diverse and frequently quarrelsome. Some advocates hold strong ideological positions, regarding corporate ownership of software code as an evil, as well as an inefficient, approach. Others are more pragmatic, regarding open source as simply a superior approach to effective software development. All, however, agree that:

> Open source (that is, software that is freely redistributed and can readily be evolved and modified to fit changing needs) is a good thing and worthy of significant and collective effort. This agreement effectively defines membership in the culture. However, the reasons individuals and various subcultures give for this belief vary considerably.[4]

This quotation comes from the work of one of the apostles of open source, Eric S. Raymond. He outlined the core principles of the movement in a manifesto essay, 'The Cathedral and the Bazaar'. In this short work he contrasts the cathedral approach to software development with that of the bazaar. Software that is built in the way that cathedrals proceed is 'carefully crafted by individual wizards or small bands of mages working in splendid isolation'.[5] In this closed model, an early version of software would not be released but would be developed by a handful of in-house technicians. The Linux community by contrast 'seemed to resemble a great babbling bazaar of different agendas and approaches...out of which a coherent and stable system could seemingly emerge only by a succession of miracles'.[6] Successful software did, however, emerge, and Raymond and others are confident that the 'severe effort of many converging wills' is more effective than the principle of command.

What value does the approach that underpins open source have for the transition of training and learning? Two questions need to be addressed here: first, are there areas where the 'severe effort of many converging wills' could be applied? Second, does the approach offer a real possibility or are there too many barriers to take it beyond the stage of conjecture?

The more one considers the first of these two questions, the more positive one becomes. The differences between learning at work and software development suggest that in fact it is learning at work that is the more promising for an approach based on shared building of information.

Software models are more absolute and precise than learning and training models. In software development, problems can be well defined and solutions generic. In training in organisations, solutions (which is not a word preferred by trainers) are tentative and situational. Training is not an exact science and we proceed pragmatically. Hence the information we share will be of the form 'I tried this and it worked for me in this situation'. This means that the sharing of information amongst trainers can proceed without a need to agree on what the most appropriate or 'correct' model for development is. By contrast, the need for agreed solutions presents a real problem in open-source software. If different schools of thought choose to develop the source, basic software programmes in different ways, there is a danger of fragmentation and losing the underlying benefits of the approach. This is graphically known as 'forking', and much energy is required of open-source developers to ensure that it does not occur. In training, by contrast, we can allow Mao's 'hundred flowers to bloom' and 'a hundred schools of thought to contend'. What is essential is a commitment to share best practice and be honest about our experiences.

All of us involved in encouraging and promoting learning at work recognise that there are issues to be addressed that would benefit from a multiplicity of perspectives. These issues will become more urgent and the problems more acute as training migrates from the classroom to the personal computer. Quite simply, we do not know enough about when, where and how people will learn best under these circumstances. We need to revisit learning styles and preferences. We need to cross boundaries. We need to build frameworks and templates that will assist trainers and learners in the workplace. Those who are undertaking academic research need to make sure that it is accessible to those who have to implement change and assist the learner. We must combine in redefining learner support.

'...e-learning demands fresh thinking and allows us to make a new start. What is hoped is that the "severe effort of many converging wills" will feature prominently in this stage of transition.'

A more difficult issue concerns the second question introduced earlier. Is this approach of building and sharing across boundaries a real possibility or are there too many barriers in the way? Time alone will answer this question. However, any blocking forces arise from cultural issues rather than systems and technology. Knowledge management techniques and the use of software tools known as groupware are now well established and encourage the shared approach to development. The barriers are ones of attitude and motivation coupled with an undue respect for institutional boundaries. It is time that we learned from each other.

To the future

In summary, e-learning demands fresh thinking and allows us to make a new start. What is hoped is that the 'severe effort of many converging wills' will feature prominently in this stage of transition. Although the phrase is taken from Russian anarchist literature, this is not to advocate anarchy: it is to say that those who believe in effective learning at work have a unique opportunity. We can practise what we preach and share knowledge and expose problems and seek joint solutions in ways that assist learners.

This manifesto for a new approach to promoting learning recognises the power of the market forces in the training industry. This recognition does not deny the legitimacy of any ethical stance. If we believe, for whatever reason, that learning matters, then working across boundaries to ease transitions and assist the disadvantaged is important. The new technologies underpinning knowledge management now allow us to proceed as a community. We have a unique opportunity to build something of lasting value.

Endnotes

1 The distinction between the terms 'learning' and 'training' can be stated as follows. Learning lies in the domain of the individual: it is about the process of changing patterns of behaviour. Training lies in the domain of the organisation: it is an intervention designed to improve the knowledge and skills of employees.

2 Department of Trade and Industry/Confederation of British Industry (1994) *Competitiveness: How the best UK companies are winning*. London, The Stationery Office.

3 On the open-source movement, see: http://release1.edventure.com/index.cfm; www.gnu.org/philosophy; and www.opensource.org/. See also: Moody, G. (2001) *Rebel Code*. London, Allen Lane Penguin Press.

4 Raymond, Eric S. (1999) *The Cathedral and the Bazaar*. Connecticut, O'Reilly. p82.

5 Ibid, p29.

6 Ibid, p30.